33 Day Family Consecration Coloring Book

Preface

This coloring book is truly the work of God. At Your Holy Family ministries, everything we undertake as a project is designed to minister to the whole family. The 33 day family consecration is designed to help each member of a family to grow closer to the Lord and closer to the other members of their family. We searched for existing coloring pages and found very little that was suitable for our consecration book. I contacted various artists to see if they might be interested in creating a few pages for our book, perhaps one per week. Imagine my surprise when one of the artists agreed not only to let us use her existing materials, but agreed to create any additional pages we needed to have one coloring page for each day.

I cannot express how much of a pleasure it was to work with R. Miller on this project. She is a very prayerful and gifted artist. I thank our Blessed Mother for bringing her to us. We couldn't have completed this project without her.

- Allen A. Hébert - Founder Your Holy Family Ministries

A Note From the Artist, R. Miller

I couldn't have done this project without the help of the Blessed Mother. I usually get anxious about commissions. Having to do a project that I didn't imagine on my own often leaves me feeling mentally paralyzed. It is hard to imagine the picture in someone else's mind. My solution was to do the Consecration myself and to pray to the Blessed Mother to inspire me. And she did! With this project I have had no trouble mentally seeing what to draw. The ideas just came one after the other. She also helped me to stay focused. I have never had an experience like this. I am so thankful that Mary, Our Mother, has been there with me all along. She is the real one to credit!

- R. Miller - Artist
www.ImmaculateHeartColoringPages.wordpress.com

For more information about Your Holy Family Ministries, please visit out website at:
www.YourHolyFamily.com

In our efforts to help families to grow in holiness, we offer retreats for the whole family, a parish-based family formation program, and workshops on family life.

Copyright © August 2015   Broussard Press
1-713-701-7007 ● www.BroussardPress.com
ISBN 978-0-9965980-26
Printed in the United States of America

Saint Anne and Saint Joachim

THE MERCY OF GOD

© 2015 R.MILLER

THE FALL OF ADAM AND EVE

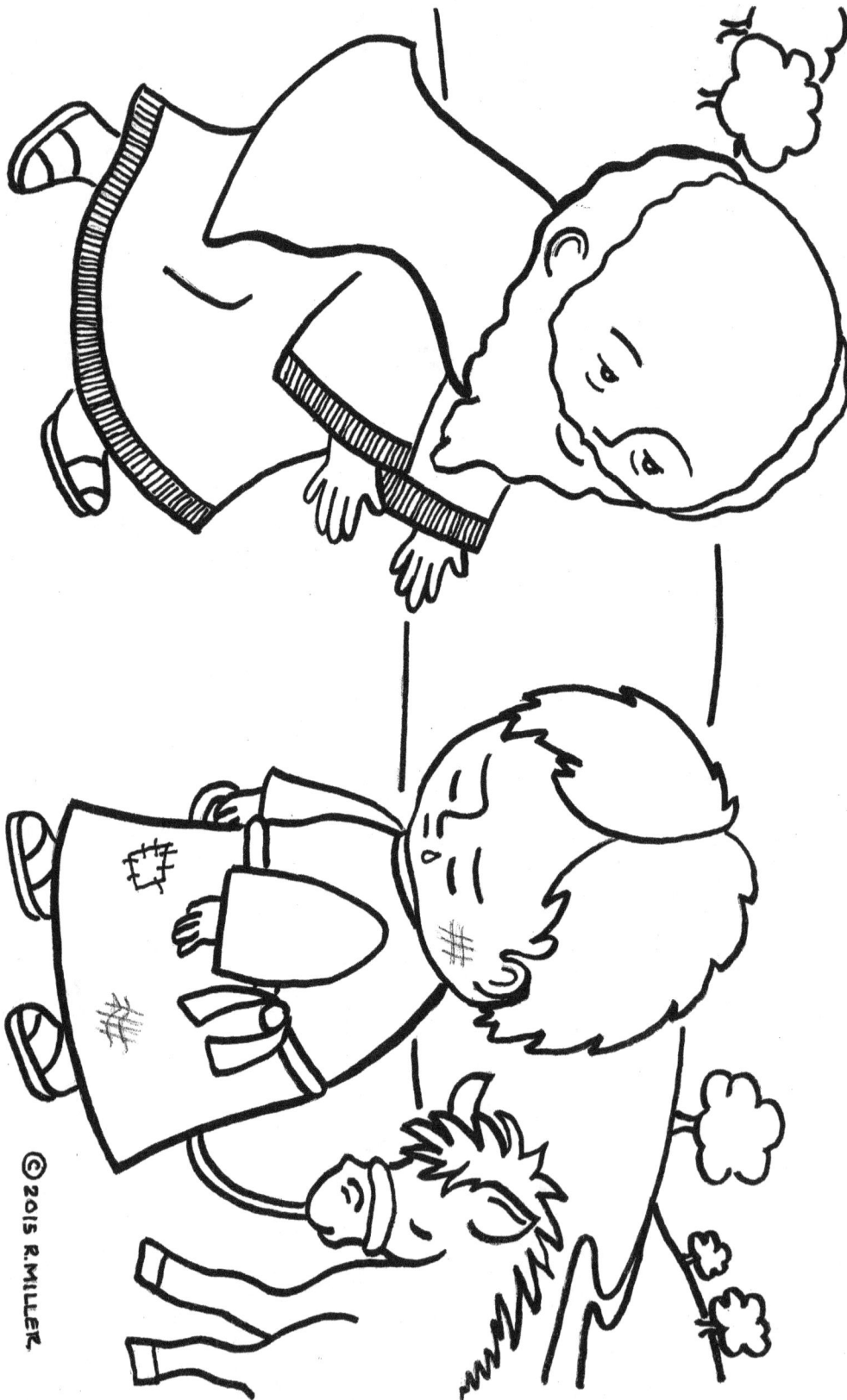

The Prodigal Son

Mary, God's Masterpiece

All Love Is From God

MARY IS LIKE THE MOON.

© 2015 R. MILLER

SHE REFLECTS THE LIGHT OF HER SON.

The Family That Prays Together Stays Together

Fr. Patrick Peyton, C.S.C.

© 2015 R. MILLER

Saint Patrick

Father

Holy Spirit

Son

© 2015 R. MILLER

© 2015 R. MILLER

The Nativity

The Annunciation

© 2015 R.MILLER

©2015 R. MILLER

THE VISITATION

Loving Our Enemies

Abraham, Sarah and Isaac

© 2015 R. MILLER

Mary At The Foot Of The Cross

Christ Has Conquered Death

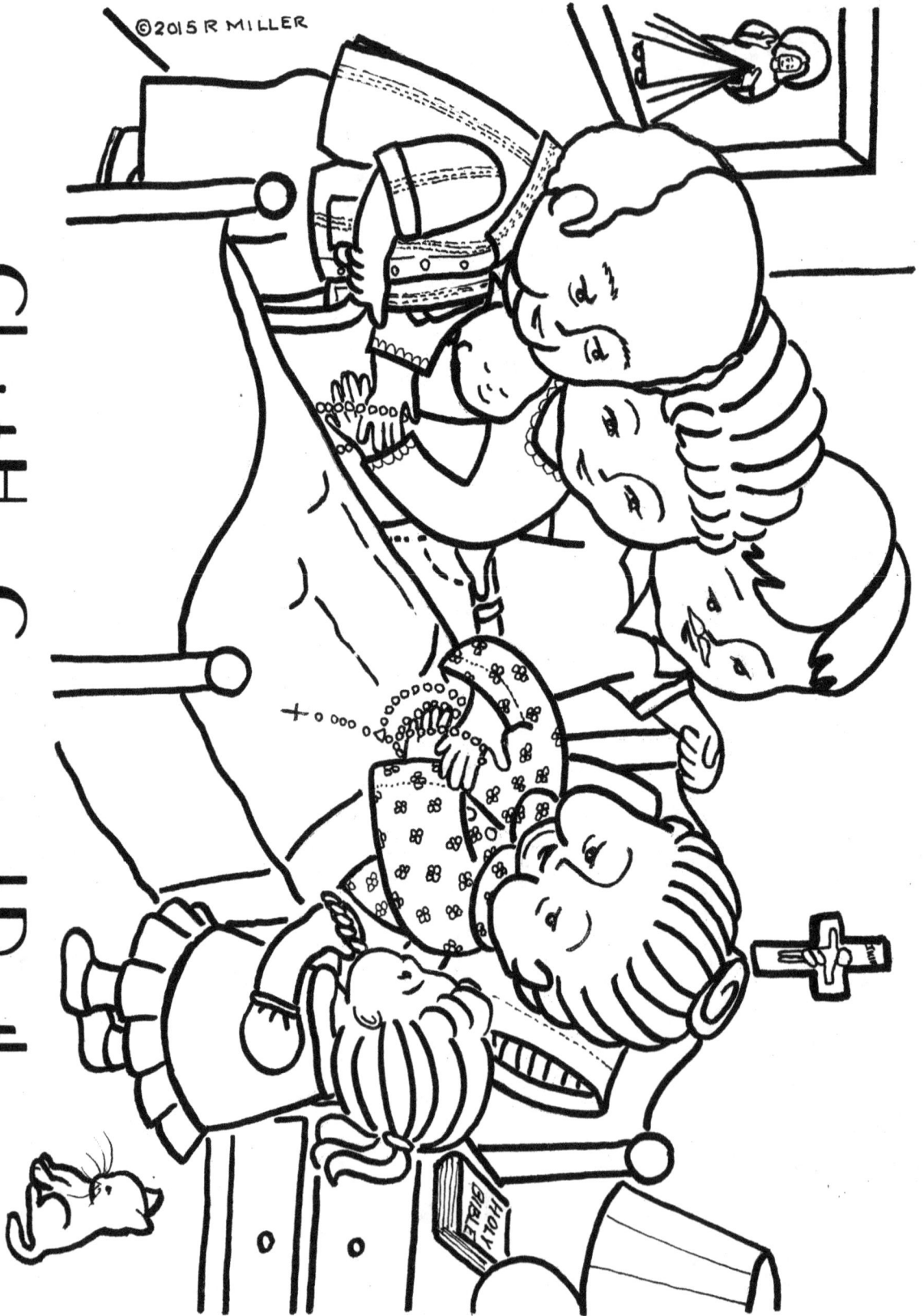

Today's Special

double scoop CHERRY GARCIA $3.95

The Glory Gate

Being Proud of Your Faith

©2015 R. Miller

Saint Longinus

© 2015 R. MILLER

The Finding of Jesus in the Temple

©2015 R MILLER

Mary the Mother of God

Mary, Queen Of All Saints

© 2015 R. Miller

Put out into the deep.

LISTENING IN SILENCE

©2015 R. MILLER

PENTECOST

© 2015 R. MILLER

Our Lady of Guadalupe

The Assumption of Mary

Saint Joseph and Jesus

©2015 R. Miller

Saint Therese
of Lisieux

© 2015 R.Miller

Pope Saint John Paul II

Follow the Lamb with Mary

We Give Our Hearts to Mary

Consecration Day Coloring Page

© 2015 R. Miller

St. Anne and St. Joachim

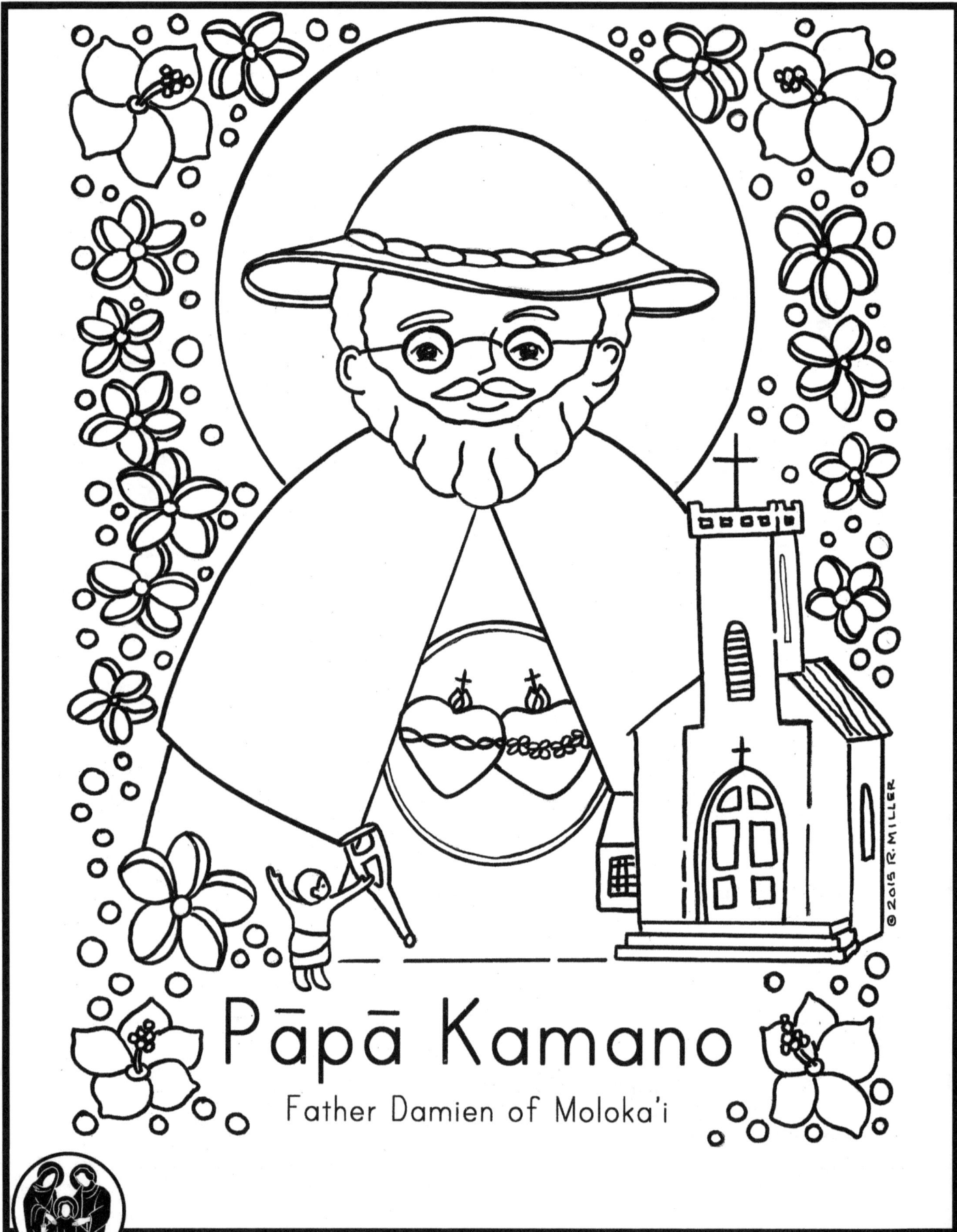

Pāpā Kamano

Father Damien of Moloka'i

Mary, Beloved of God

Mother Teresa
of Calcutta

God Loves A Cheerful Giver

2 Corinthians 9:7

www.ingramcontent.com/pod-product-compliance
Lightning Source LLC
Chambersburg PA
CBHW080216040426

42331CB00035B/3143